A New Way Home

a personalised approach to leaving institutions

Scottish Edition

by **Frances Brown and John Dalrymple**

Published by the Centre for Welfare Reform in association with Citizen Network

Contents

Centre for Welfare Reform

Preface

'... the difficulty of bringing people back home once they have been placed a long way away is so great that every effort should be made to avoid such placements.'

Mansell, 2007

That place of great difficulty is where this guide starts.

People with learning disabilities and challenging behaviour have continued to be placed in long-stay institutions, often a long way from home. New 'placements' of this kind have not always been avoided, and some people have not yet been afforded the opportunity to plan for their departure.

Yet the urgency of the need to help people make their journey home is undiminished. They are not living in safe surroundings. Jim Mansell understood this too. When news of the scandal at Winterbourne View first broke, and some were assuming that it might reflect a problem specific to that particular institution, he was clear in his analysis:

'The real solution... is to stop using these kinds of places altogether. Who will hold local health and social services to account to make that happen?'

Mansell, 2011

This travel guide demonstrates tried and trusted methods for navigating the difficult road home. (The guide demonstrating how to avoid that difficult journey in the first place is perhaps for another day, though its outline can be discerned from the principles and practices described here.) But it also affords all of us, as concerned citizens, a set of principles, ideas and practices we can use to hold each other to account in making sure these journeys are taken.

5

Introduction

An earlier version of this publication was set in the context of *Building the right support* (NHS England, ADASS, Local Government Association 2015) a national plan to develop community services in England and close inpatient facilities for people with a learning disability and/or autism who display challenging behaviour. The context for this Scottish version is provided by two relatively recent reports.

The first is the Mental Welfare Commission's *No Through Road* report of 2016 on the circumstances of people with learning disabilities living in hospital. Its major finding was that 32% of those people were experiencing very significant delays in their discharge from hospital. The main reasons cited for these delays were "lack of funding, accommodation, or an appropriate care provider; or a combination of these issues".

The subsequent *Coming Home* (Scottish Government, 2018) report identified a total of 705 people from Scotland "with learning disabilities and complex needs", aged 16 or over, who had been affected by "delayed discharge" from hospital and/or were living in "out-of-area placements", as at 31st January, 2017. Of this total, 45% had already been living "out of area" for more than 10 years; 23% for more than 5 years. Seventy-nine individuals (11.2%) were living in hospitals in England and Wales. In seeking to address identified gaps in knowledge, competence and infrastructure found at various levels of the national system of services for people with these "complex" requirements, the report recommended developing commissioning and service planning; and workforce development in positive behavioural support.

These reports emphasise the fact that people with learning disabilities and challenging behaviour are especially vulnerable to the possibility of having to move away from home. Their behaviour is judged to be highly risky to themselves and to others, and their removal from home to segregated institutions is often regarded as the 'safe' option. Indeed the term challenging behaviour was originally coined to highlight the fact that the 'behaviours' under discussion are as much 'challenges' to the service system as they are to the person and those around them. In other words,

challenging behaviour is not only risky for the wellbeing of the person exhibiting it, but also invites a segregated, institutional, out-of-area response from the social care system:

'Severely challenging behaviour refers to behaviour of such an intensity, frequency or duration that the physical safety of the person or others is likely to be placed in serious jeopardy, or behaviour which is likely to seriously limit or delay access to and use of ordinary community facilities.'

Emerson, 2011

This suggests a very significant double jeopardy. People exhibiting challenging behaving do present many real risks to themselves and others. The danger of physical harm and injury. Risks that their mental health may be damaged or that mental illness may be an underlying factor in prompting the behaviour. Risks that they may commit the types of offences that range from physical assault to matters of more 'forensic' concern.

But removal from home on the grounds of seeking to minimise these risks brings with it real and present threats to life: institutionalisation; segregation; significant loss of power and control; stigmatisation and blame; physical and sexual abuse; years of wasted time; exclusion from society and from the cash economy; and exposure to levels of administrative complexity which render effective communication and person-centred future planning extremely difficult.

For people associated with these levels of exclusion, confusion and perceived risk it may become difficult to even begin to envisage what a positive future might look like (see Figure 1). It is the purpose of this guide to help rectify that situation.

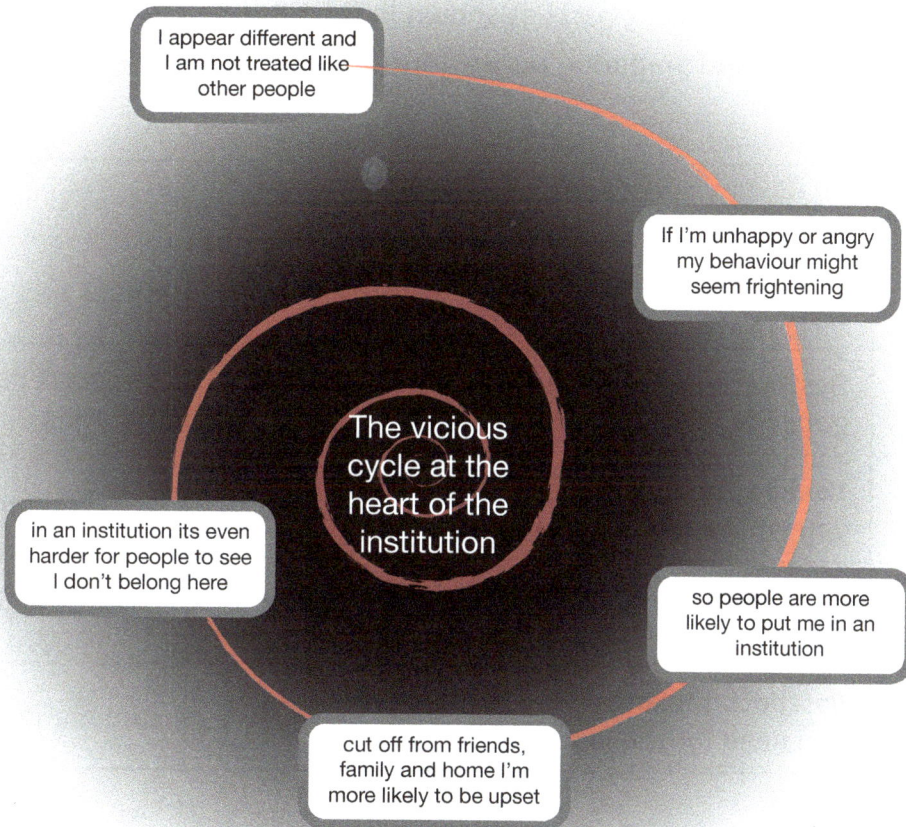

FIGURE 1. THE VICIOUS CYCLE AT THE HEART OF THE INSTITUTION

The Guide

This guide is organised into 5 parts as shown in the table below. Each part represents a stage in planning and preparing for the journey ahead.

Part	Stage	Content
1	**Compass:** getting our bearings before we start	values and principles
2	**Destination:** your picture of home, and a good life	person-centred planning
3	**Vehicle:** taking control of the support that you will need to live your life	self-directed support
4	**Road Map:** directions for the help you will need back home	support planning
5	**Passport:** making sure you have everything you need for the journey	care management

Part 1 of the guide is addressed to all of us, whatever part we play in our shared humanity to making these journeys happen.

Parts 2-5 are addressed to the individual man or woman making the journey home. This does not mean that it is considered to be 'easy-read', or readily 'accessible', but it does imply that anyone using the guide to assist people complete their journey should consistently be reminded whose journey this is, and whose choices and preferences ultimately count.

In the **Afterword** we remind ourselves of our vital shared responsibility to hold each other to account: to ensure that in future people are not displaced from their homes and institutionalised; and to ensure that those already displaced are brought back home as speedily as possible.

The guide also includes some examples of important documents that you may want to use as you work together.

Example document	Part
Rachael's Personal Plan: information about Rachael and her plans for the future	**2 Destination**
Rachael's Individual Service Fund: a breakdown of the support costs for Rachael	**3 Vehicle**
The Smith Family: a detailed case study of a family who used an individual service fund	**4 Road Map**
Housing Specification: questions you need to think about when looking for a new home	**4 Road Map**
Thomas's Transition Plan: a plan for helping someone move out of institutional care	**4 Road Map**

REFERENCES

Emerson E (1995) cited in Emerson E (2001, 2nd edition): *Challenging Behaviour: Analysis and intervention in people with learning disabilities.* Cambridge, Cambridge University Press.

Mansell J (2007) *Services for people with learning disabilities and challenging behaviour or mental health needs.* London, Department of Health.

Mansell J (2011) *Bristol care home: a failure on every level* in The Guardian 1st June, 2011.

Mental Welfare Commission for Scotland (2016) *No Through Road: People with Learning Disabilities in Hospital.* Edinburgh, Mental Welfare Commission.

NHS England, ADASS, Local Government Association (2015) *Building the right support: A national plan to develop community services and close inpatient facilities for people with a learning disability and/or autism who display behaviour that challenges, including those with a mental health condition.* London, NHS England.

Scottish Government (2018) *Coming Home: A Report on Out-of-Area Placements and Delayed Discharge for People with Learning Disabilities and Complex Needs.* Edinburgh, Scottish Government.

Compass

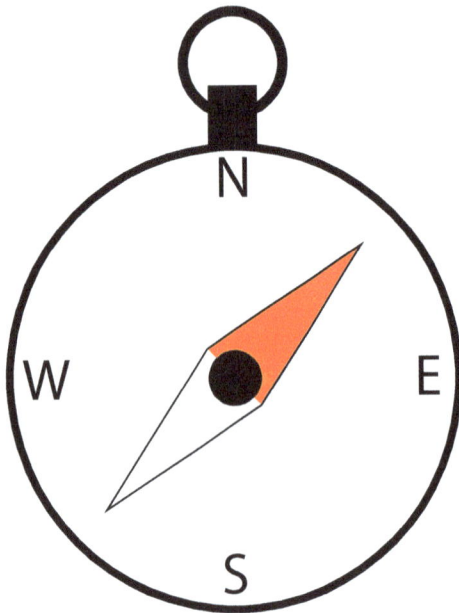

Centre for Welfare Reform

1. Compass

The public perception of people with learning disability and challenging behaviour is a negative one:

- their disabilities, in and of themselves, cause them to be misunderstood, undervalued, viewed as different;
- the behaviours they display create fear and anxiety, a perception of irrational violence, and a desire that they should be kept at a distance;
- in turn, the segregation and institutionalisation that often follow merely add to the associated fear and stigma.

People with learning disability and challenging behaviour and who live in institutions are therefore considered to be dangerous, diminished people, who present major risks to themselves and to others, and are perhaps best kept separate and segregated for their own good and for the benefit of the community. This perception of risk certainly extends to the matter of helping people return from home from institutions. On all sorts of different levels it's seen to be a risky business and often for that reason not worth embarking upon.

Status not stigma

In light of this general perception, therefore, it's important to assert from the outset that people with learning disability or autism who display challenging behaviour are not only 'worth the risk'; but that they are entitled to be seen as men and women with full and equal adult status, whose behaviour should be understood as an attempt to communicate something important about their predicament, and whose requirements for personal fulfilment are no different from anyone else.

It is also important to assert that the risks their behaviours pose to themselves and to others are risks that can be managed in local, community settings. There is nothing intrinsic to their behaviour, or the risks this behaviour creates, which implies they are better managed in large institutions, far from home – indeed the opposite is true

(Mansell, 2007). Nor is it acceptable to argue that the large institutions are required in order to manage the behaviours of a small number of people who are said to be exceptions to this rule – we have known for a long time that for each person living in an institutional setting there is an equivalent person, with similar characteristics, living well in the community (Baker & Urquhart, 1987).

Navigation

So to make sure we don't get lost or stranded along the way, we need to take out our compass and get some proper bearings before we set out on this journey. And just as a compass helps us to position ourselves by pointing to Magnetic North, we will take our bearings from five 'north stars', or principles to which we can refer for guidance as we undertake the journey, and for assistance when we fear we may be getting lost. Because, in light of the negative perception of the people concerned, and the distorted understanding of the risks that they pose, it will be important at every stage of the journey to remember that:

- we all share a set of common human needs
- we are all unique and individual
- we all have equal status and value
- we must all make decisions about our own lives
- we all live life in and through our relationships

We all share a set of common human needs

The first and most fundamental starting point is that, universally and without distinction, human beings share a set of common needs. Throughout our lives we all need security, love, relationships, a sense of purpose.

The most famous definition of our common human needs was offered by Maslow, who identified (see Figure 2):

- first, our basic physiological needs (for food, water, warmth and rest)
- then, our need for security and safety
- next, our need to belong and to experience love through intimate relationships with other people
- followed by, our need for self-esteem—to be able to be confident in our own achievements and to have the respect of other people
- finally, the need for a sense of fulfilment and purpose in our lives.

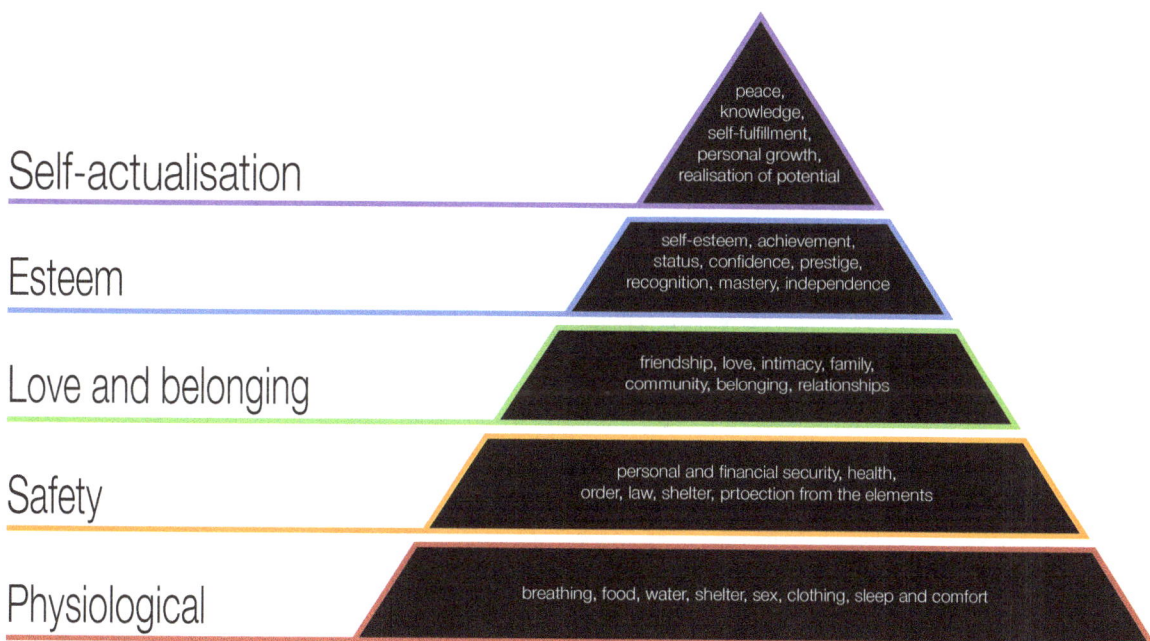

Self-actualisation — peace, knowledge, self-fulfillment, personal growth, realisation of potential

Esteem — self-esteem, achievement, status, confidence, prestige, recognition, mastery, independence

Love and belonging — friendship, love, intimacy, family, community, belonging, relationships

Safety — personal and financial security, health, order, law, shelter, prtoection from the elements

Physiological — breathing, food, water, shelter, sex, clothing, sleep and comfort

FIGURE 2. MASLOW'S HEIRARCHY OF NEED

One practical application of Maslow's definition is the framework devised by Simon Duffy in *Keys to Citizenship*. We will refer to this framework in various sections of this guide.

It describes seven conditions that need to be met in order for any of us to live fulfilling lives as citizens in our communities (see Figure 3):

1. **Meaning** - purpose and direction in our lives
2. **Freedom** -personal control of our own affairs
3. **Money** - enough cash to sustain our independence
4. **Home** - a private place where we belong
5. **Help** - the support and assistance of others
6. **Life** - opportunities to contribute to our communities
7. **Love** - reciprocal friendships and intimate relationships

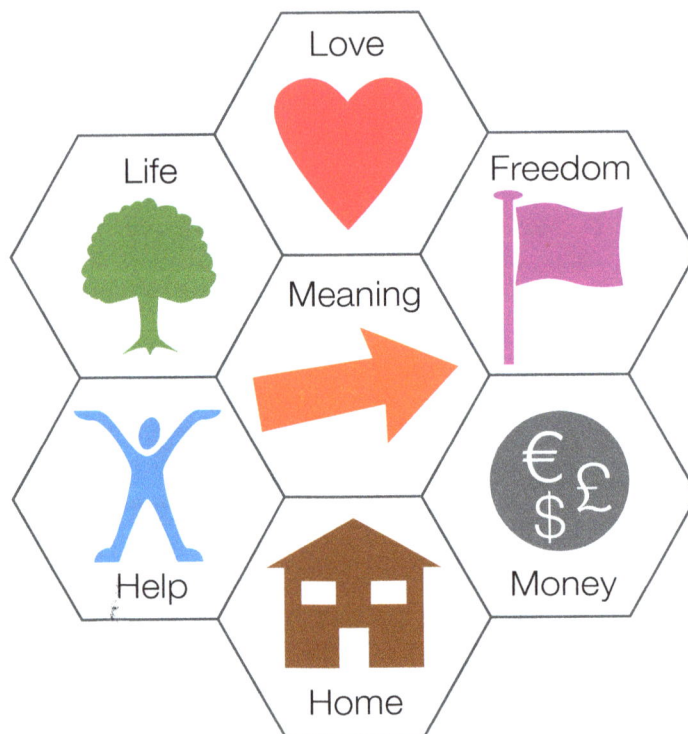

FIGURE 3. THE 7 KEYS TO CITIZENSHIP

These are not just things that some people need and others can do without. And there certainly isn't a set of special needs reserved for people with disabilities or people who display challenging behaviour. What is different for people with disabilities is that they very often need additional amounts of help from others in

order to ensure that their basic human needs are met. And sometimes this translates into the specialist type of paid support that some people with disabilities require to help sustain their lives.

In the same way, disability is not a condition that people carry about within themselves. It exists in the space where the person interacts with the social world and the physical environment. Disability is not an illness to be cured, therefore, but rather people with disabilities often need assistance to reduce the restrictions they encounter in the world as they seek to live their lives.

> We share a common humanity uncompromised by the extent of any disability or disadvantage we have, undiluted by any requirement we have for additional help and support.

We are all unique and individual

While we all share a set of common needs, we are each at the same time unique people. We are all the same and yet we are all different. These are not opposing ideas, but instead they are complementary.

Each of us is human; each of us, without exception, is genetically and biochemically unique.

Psychologically, we are all different too. We develop our own personal preferences, our likes and dislikes, our own personal dreams and ambitions for our person life. We take joy and satisfaction from distinct aspects of life, but can also identify those things for which we have no appetite. If I love jazz and have mere contempt for macaroni cheese it may feel as though I have little in common with my neighbours and friends, but these expressions of my personality do not render me any less human. Maslow suggests that we all seek to develop and preserve a 'psychological freedom' that does not require validation by someone or something outwith ourselves. We dare to be different even if that means we come into conflict with the communities we live in.

The uniqueness of each person, and the great diversity this implies, sits in opposition therefore to the tendency to view people with disabilities as a homogenous class of human beings with undifferentiated needs, wants and aspirations – people who can be 'grouped' or 'clustered', and whose personal preferences are of little account. At each stage it will be important to ensure that the personality of the person making the journey home is fully reflected in all that it is done.

> Our claim to our own unique personality is not determined by an assessment of any deficits we are perceived to have, but is upheld by the mere fact of our humanity.

Each of us is of equal status and value

As unique people sharing a common humanity, we all share an equal status and value as human beings. Considerations of gender, wealth, sexuality, age etc cannot diminish the value and status of the person as a person, nor make one person subordinate to another (except in the legal status of children with respect to adults).

International law supports and defends this position by means of landmark agreements such as the *Universal Declaration of Human Rights* (1948) and the *European Convention on Human Rights* (1953). The *Human Rights Act* (1998) incorporated the rights conferred by the European Convention into British law. The UK is also a signatory to the *United Nations Convention on the Rights of People with Disabilities* (2006), although its provisions have not to date been incorporated into domestic law.

It is therefore not acceptable for any actual our perceived limitation of the intellectual capacity of a person with challenging behaviour to be used as a justification for denying that person:

- The right to **life**
- Freedom from **torture** and **inhuman** or **degrading treatment**
- Freedom from **slavery** and **forced labour**
- The right to **liberty** and **security**

- The right to a **fair trial**
- The right to **no punishment without law**
- Respect for **private** and **family life**, **home** and **correspondence**
- Freedom of **thought**, **belief** and **religion**
- Freedom of **expression**
- Freedom of **assembly** and **association**
- The right to **marry** and **start a family**

Indeed Article 14 of the *European Convention on Human Rights* specifically states that people have the right to be protected from discrimination in respect of these rights and freedoms.

Our claim that all human beings have equal value and status is confirmed by right within international and domestic law. It is illegal to treat me as less than human, or to treat me as less significant or important than other human beings, on account of any disability I might have.

We must all make decisions about our own lives

Reasons of reduced intellectual capacity are also used to justify the practice of making choices and decisions for people with challenging behaviour. An assumption is made that people lack the capacity to make decisions for themselves and so require others to make decisions for them.

Yet, if we all share a common humanity, a unique personality and an equal status and value then it is essential for each one of us to take as many of the decisions that affect our own lives as possible. At the very least, to have as much input as possible into the decisions that affect our lives.

The *United Nations Convention on the Rights of Persons with Disabilities* sets a clear expectation that signatories (including the UK) *"shall take appropriate steps to provide access by persons with disabilities to the support they may require in exercising their legal capacity"*.

In this sense it is important to realise that "legal capacity" is not the same thing as decision-making capacity. A person's decision-making capacity relates to their ability to make decisions about things that affect their life. To have decision-making capacity means that the person can understand a decision, the available choices, the consequences of any decision they make and can communicate this decision.

"Legal capacity" on the other hand is the ability to hold rights and to make decisions that are respected and capable of being enforced under the law (e.g. signing contracts and agreeing to medical care and treatment). Some people have impaired decision-making capacity or, in extreme cases (for example, a person in a coma) may have no decision-making capacity at all. But the UNCRPD, 2006 states that everyone with a disability should enjoy *"legal capacity on an equal basis with others in all aspects of life"*. For that to happen, they need support – either to help them make a decision for themselves or, if that is genuinely not possible, to ensure that a decision is made on their behalf which respects their rights, will and preferences (see Figure 4).

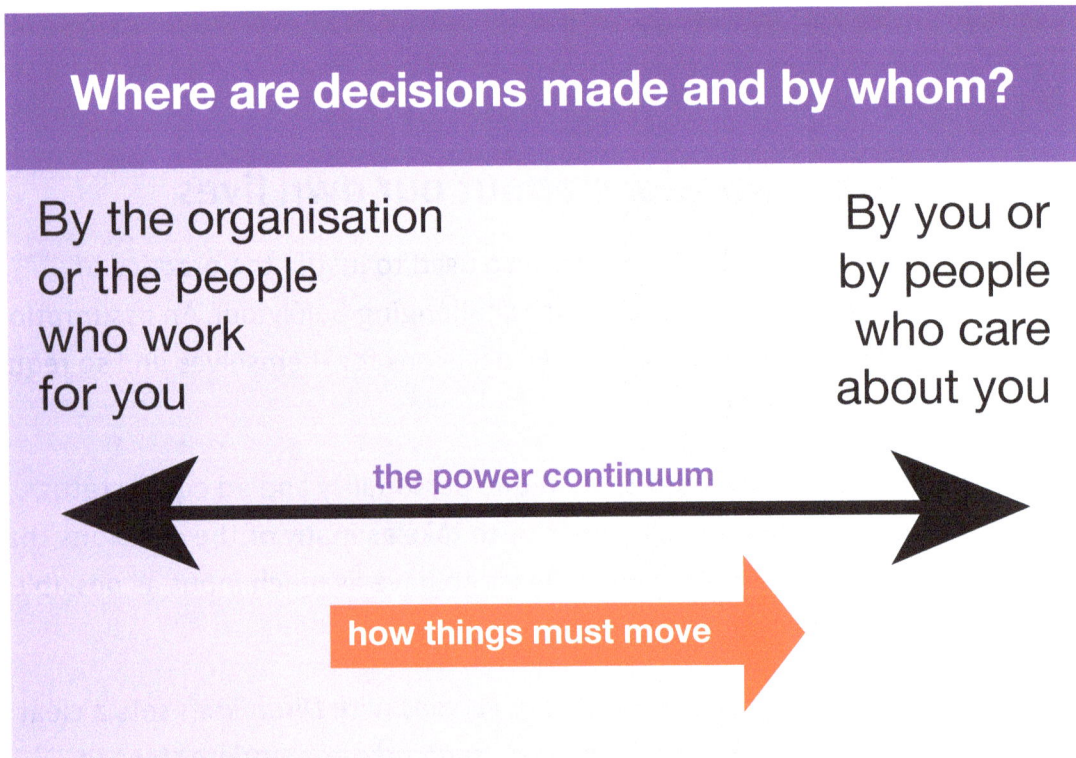

Where are decisions made and by whom?

By the organisation or the people who work for you

By you or by people who care about you

the power continuum

how things must move

FIGURE 4. MOVING TO EMPOWERMENT

This concept of supported decision-making can be used to refer to any process in which a person is provided with as much support as they need in order for them to be able to: make a decision for themselves; and/or express their will and preferences within the context of substitute decision-making (for example, guardianship or compulsory treatment for mental disorder). In both cases, the purpose of supported decision-making is to ensure that the person's will and preferences are central to and fully respected in decisions that concern them.

In all of this it is important to understand that each person with challenging behaviour is different and needs to be seen in the context of a continuum that reflects a greater or lesser need for support in decision-making. It is also the case that different people will sometimes require differing levels of support for different types of decisions (e.g. making decisions about financial matters may require more support than making decisions about what to eat and drink).

The Mental Welfare Commission's good practice guide on supported decision-making (2017) fully supports these principles and describes ways in which they can be put into practice.

> Each of us has the same legal capacity as each other in all aspects of our lives and each of us requires the appropriate level and type of support in decision-making that will allow us to sustain our legal capacity, no matter how severe our disability.

We all live life in and through our relationships

As unique individuals of equal value and status, our need for personal control over the decisions which affect our lives is counterbalanced by our need to have rewarding relationships of give-and-take with each other. The quality of our human connection, one to another, forms the basis of our sense of security in the world and is the source of our emotional fulfilment – the place where we give and receive love, affection, nurture and support. This is true at the intimate level of one-to-one personal and family relationships and also at the less intense, more social level of our relationships

with people in our local neighbourhoods and communities: we make sense of the world, and our place within it, through other people. So much so that, as studies have shown, the more limited our range of relationships with other people - the more isolated we become and the more lonely we feel - the more likely we are to die prematurely (Holt-Lunstad, 2015).

For people with learning disabilities and challenging behaviour, who for various social reasons are from the outset of their lives much more likely than the average citizen to be isolated within their communities, or segregated from them, this issue is thus all the more acute. Not only must we do everything in our power to prevent their removal to long-stay institutions in the first place; but we must also make sure that in helping people plan their journey home we pay full and proper attention to the range and quality of relationships they are able to enjoy on their return.

We all need each other. Interpersonal relationships are vital to our personal development. Serious constrictions in our relationships undermine our health and well-being and are ultimately life-threatening. This is no less true for people with learning disabilities and challenging behaviour who are already much more likely to be marginalised in society and face the risk of losing relationships through institutionalisation. Ensuring people with learning disability and challenging behaviour have people in their lives is of the utmost importance.

REFERENCES

Baker N and Urquhart N (1987) *The Balance of Care for Adults with a Learning Disability in Scotland.* Edinburgh, Scottish Office, ISD Publications.

ECHR (1950) *European Convention on Human Rights.*

Duffy S (2006) *The Keys to Citizenship.* 2nd edition. Sheffield, Centre for Welfare Reform.

Holt-Lunstad J et al (2015) *Loneliness and Social Isolation as Risk Factors for Mortality: A Meta-Analytic Review,* PERSPECTIVES ON PSYCHOLOGICAL SCIENCE, Vol 10(2), pp227-237.

Mansell J (2007) *Services for people with learning disabilities and challenging behaviour or mental health needs*. London, Department of Health.

Maslow A H (1943) *A Theory of Human Motivation*. PSYCHOLOGICAL REVIEW, 50(4), 370-96.

Mental Welfare Commission for Scotland (2017) *Good Practice Guide: Supported Decision Making*. Edinburgh, Mental Welfare Commission.

UDHR (1948) *Universal Declaration of Human Rights*.

UK Government (1998) *Human Rights Act*:

UNCRPD (2006) *Convention on the Rights of Persons with Disabilities*.

Destination

2. Destination

If you are starting out on this journey it is because at some point in the past you have been moved away from your family and community, and you are presently living in a segregated institutional setting some distance from home. In order to begin this journey, you need to have some idea of what the future might hold for you, a good idea of where you are headed, and what your ultimate destination will be. You need *"a compelling image of a desirable future"* and you need to *"invite people to join with you to make it happen"* (O'Brien & Lovett, 1992). This is the essence of a person-centred approach.

So let's think about how you could draw this **picture of the future you would like to have**, what some people have called a **Life Plan**.

Create a picture of your future

First of all, this is **your** picture. It's the picture of the life **you** would like to have. Though you may at various stages require some assistance in sketching it out, it must be drawn from, and reflect, **your** point of view. Whatever else it does it should capture **your desires and wishes for your own future**. And it should do so in a way that leaves other people in no doubt about what they are.

The picture of the future you desire should therefore:

- be clear and easily understood;
- be specific to you as an individual;
- bring your unique personality to life;
- pay attention to all the key things that will allow you to have a full life;
- provide a strong foundation to inform future actions and decisions.

Centre for Welfare Reform

Invite people to join you

To make sure that you are able to draw the clearest picture, it is important that you gather round you all the important people in your life. You will know who these people are. Members of your **family**, most likely, other **friends**, perhaps.

You also have the right to identify the **professional people** you want to be involved - like social workers, community nurses, independent advocates, service brokers, etc., who may have been given the specific job of working with you to help you make this journey.

You also need to know that there are people around the country, in different organisations, who are available to help you draw this picture. It can be a great help to have an **independent** facilitator with lots of experience, good at helping you and all the people who are important to you, to take part in the best way possible to help build up your personal plan. A number of organisations in different parts of Scotland are able to help in this way. Check the websites of Citizen Network, In Control Scotland and Person Centred Planning Network Scotland for more information.

Gather vital information

There are a number of different ways to go about gathering the information that will form the basis of your picture and a number of different tools you can use (Ritchie, 1997). Often people will make use of a number of different tools and methods to make sure that everything gets captured, and the plan is as robust as possible:

- you can record your own account; and/or
- you can work closely with a facilitator who will get to know you really well on a one-to-one basis; and/or
- the facilitator can have a series of conversations with you and other important people in your life – family, friends, peers, professionals who know you really well (or sometimes want to get to know you better); and/or
- the facilitator can gather you and all the others together in a group where everyone can share the information that they have.

Document the information you need

The information that is gathered will need to be recorded. It can be recorded in a variety of ways:

- using words that are easily understood;
- using graphics or pictures that bring the picture to life;
- using video and audio clips.

It will take time and commitment for people to work with you to build up this picture. It's not something that can be rushed. People need to go at a pace you are comfortable with. But, there is also no time to be wasted, especially if you are living in a situation you are unhappy with and are keen to change.

Frame the picture

As the process draws to a close, the information needs to be pulled into a shape and a format that you can share with everyone concerned and everyone who might be involved along the way. The facilitator will keep track of the things people agree about, as well as the things that people disagree about, and might need further discussion. There is no set format, and no particular style that your plan must follow – it's best if it's written in a way that matches who you are, using words and pictures and any other approaches that help. It is important to make sure, however, that the picture is rich and full, containing information about everything other people might need to know about how you see the future.

A possible framework

Your own life story

What has happened to you up this point? This should include:

- where and when you were born
- information about your family
- where you grew up
- where you went to school
- the jobs that you've had
- the various places you have lived
- how you came to be living away from home

The life you lead now

Your picture should also contain an account of the life you are living now:

- the place you are living in
- the people living there who are important to you
- the daily routines that you follow at the moment
- what works well for you at the moment
- what is not working so well

Your personal characteristics

How would you describe your own personality and what impression do other people get when they meet you? What do people like and admire about you?

Your unique attributes

Having a good life involves being able to share with other people:

- your gifts
- your skills
- your strengths
- your interests

Your relationships to other people

The people in your life who are able to help you grow and develop, who love and support you:

- your family
- your friends
- your peers
- your colleagues

Your sense of what home means to you

You will need a house to live in when you get back home. But having your own house does not translate automatically into having a place you can genuinely call home:

- a house is not a home unless you can relax and be at ease within it, unless you can shut the door behind you and 'make yourself at home';
- your house will not be your home unless you are able to connect to it emotionally, and to invest something of yourself within it;
- otherwise a house is just a building, and you will run the danger of swapping a room in a hospital or residential unit for a few, perhaps nicer, rooms in a housing estate.

So the picture you draw will need to describe where you want to live – the village or town or city that you think of as your home. This might be the town where you were born and grew up, or it might be the community where your family, or the people you feel closest to emotionally, are currently living. You might also have to be clear about which specific part of a larger town or city you might want to live in.

The picture you draw will also need to let people know if you prefer the thought of having your home to yourself, or if you would prefer to live with other people you know and love. It may be that someone you are close to would like you to go to live in their house, and you might be attracted to this idea, but you should be under no compulsion to live with another person, or other people, if that does not fit with your picture of the future.

Your life in your community

If your house is to be your home it will need to make it easy for you to connect to the street you live in, the local neighbourhood, and the wider local community, and to mix freely with your family and neighbours and friends.

Your picture should describe the things you will need in the local community to help you stay active and healthy, and to use your gifts and skills to make a contribution.

Your desires and wishes

Your picture should paint a very clear image of all the things that you need or want to have in your life:

- it might help to start with the **things that matter most to you** - the most important things from your point of view – the things without which your life will not be worth living;
- you can then turn to the **things that are important to you** – the things you need to give your life meaning and purpose;
- and finally the plan can list the **things you enjoy or prefer to have in your life**.

The picture you draw should also try to capture your hopes for the longer term future. These might not be very clear to you at the moment and might well become much clearer once you have been back home living for a while. Nonetheless, it is good to sketch out the direction you see your life taking – the things you would like to do to give your life meaning and purpose. Perhaps, the new skills you would like to learn, the topics you would like to study at college, the job you would like to have, the kind of relationships you hope for. It's not just OK to be ambitious for your own future, it's important and healthy, so don't be shy about sharing your dreams. (And, as you prepare for this difficult journey home, you might also want to be clear about some of your **fears** about the future, so that people have a clear sense of what you are most worried about in this next stage of your life.)

REFERENCES

Pages 30-37 offer a real world example of a support plan. This plan has been shared with the permission of Rachael and her family. Other examples are available from the websites listed below.

Citizen Network https://citizen-network.org

In Control Scotland https://www.in-controlscotland.org

O'Brien J and Lovett H (1992) *Finding A Way To Ordinary Lives: The Contribution of Person-Centred Planning.* Harrisburg, Pennsylvania Office of Mental Retardation.

Person Centred Planning Network Scotland https://pcpscotland.wixsite.com/network

Radical Visions http://radicalvisions.wpengine.com

Ritchie P et al (1997) *People. Plans and Practicalities. Achieving change through person centred planning.* Edinburgh, Scottish Human Services.

Rachael's Personal Plan

Introduction

Rachael is a young woman who lives in her own flat in the town where she grew up. To fund the support that she requires, Rachael has a Direct Payment which is managed by her parents who are her legal guardians. Rachael uses this money to buy support from a service proving organisation, and has her own bespoke support team.

Rachael was recently reassessed by social work staff from the local authority, and a new budget for her support was agreed. Rachael and her parents were keen to use the new budget in the form of an Individual Service Fund, and the local authority was content that the planning process should be used as a learning experience for all concerned. There was agreement that the creation of an Individual Service Fund would permit Rachael greater flexibility and control, and allow her parents to have less responsibility for managing and accounting for the funding.

The plan is the result of a number of meetings held to help Rachael and her family think about the support they get now but also to focus on Rachael's dreams and hopes for a meaningful life and future. Currently Rachael receives a service she is happy with but which does not meet all of her changing needs and outcomes. The planning process considered the changes Rachael and her parents wanted to make in the way that the available resources are used, to ensure not only that Rachael continues to get the support she needs to stay safe and keep well, but also to consider more imaginative ways in which she could use her resources to meet her outcomes for a good and meaningful life.

People in Rachael's Life

Rachael is a young woman at the heart of her family. She lives in a beautiful flat, decorated to her taste, and she is very house proud. Her parents live really close by, and Rachael regularly spends planned time with them, and with her grandparents. In addition, Rachael sustains good relationships with a number of special friends in her community.

Rachael also has a number of important people in her life working together in a Circle of Friends. These people have been meeting regularly to support Rachael and spend time with her since she was at school. Some people have moved on and others have joined the circle over time.

The other people who are important to Rachael are the members of staff employed by the service provider specifically to support Rachael.

Who is Rachael

People who know and love Rachael describe her in the following ways:

- likes to laugh and in turn makes others laugh
- quiet at first until she gets to know the situation
- sensitive
- loves her family and friends
- a bubbly, fun person
- loves to sing and perform
- pretty, stylish and likes to look good
- organised
- likes to be in control and let you know what she wants
- a good friend
- house-proud
- caring about others
- likes to be the host
- has an amazing smile and laugh
- makes you feel good
- Rachael is fun

What matters most to Rachael

- Not noisy: Rachael likes quiet and calm
- People – mum and dad, family and friends
- Love and relationships

- The area where she stays must be safe
- Being accepted not judged
- Meeting new friends
- Keeping in touch with existing friends
- Visiting people and inviting people over to the flat
- Being able to touch animals
- A good night's sleep
- Music: Karaoke singing, and seeing herself singing
- Walking, laughing and having fun
- Encouragement to try new things, stick to plans and be motivated
- Spending time alone in the flat
- Pushing things: buggies, wheelchairs, prams

Things that are important for Rachael

It is important that Rachael is healthy and safe, and these are some of the things we talked about that would help Rachael stay safe.

- Being well known at home, with neighbours and people in the community looking out for her
- Having good neighbours who can look out for her and let us know if they are at all worried
- Assistive technology to allow Rachael to contact and talk to someone if she needs help when she is alone
- Regular use and testing of equipment in the house to make sure everything works, e.g., fire alarm
- People responding when and if needed
- Support being able to change if needed, e.g if Rachael was ill and needed someone to stay over

- Always using the door entry system
- Eating well
- Keeping fit: swimming, walking, aqua Zumba, belly dancing
- Good support to ensure safety when out and about and accessing public transport

Staying healthy and well

Rachael needs to stay healthy and well and these things will help to keep her on track:

- A healthy diet
- Drinking lots every day
- Walking
- Swimming
- Going to the park and using the swings
- Horse riding
- Exercise videos
- Wii fit sports
- Medication
- Support to make healthy choices
- Support with choices appropriate clothing for weather
- Support staff aware and following health needs as stated in MLMSP

How Rachael is supported now

Rachael currently gets support through a small team of personal assistants employed by the support organisation. Recruitment and retention have at times been difficult, leading to several changes in personnel and Rachael having to rely more on her mum, her wider family and her circle of support.

- Rachael currently has support staff each day between 9.30am and 11pm, with a change of personnel at 5pm
- Rachael has no staff during the night

- Rachael has a call system in case of emergency and has the emergency button by her bed
- Rachael currently goes to her parents' home for dinner some nights during the week
- Rachael spends the weekend (Friday night until Sunday afternoon) with her grandparents every 6-8 weeks
- Rachael sometimes spends the night with her mum and dad
- Rachael will sometimes have a member of her Circle of Friends stay overnight as she loves to have people stay over at her house

Support is paid for currently from Rachael's Direct Payment, managed by her parents, who also have welfare guardianship and help Rachael make decisions about her life and her future. The amount of the Direct Payment was reviewed recently and increased to reflect Rachael's present requirements.

Rachael has been letting staff know that she is seeking further independence, often asking staff to leave when they are on shift as she feels she needs more space. This request from Rachael has to be balanced with the need to keep her safe and make sure that she is able to get access to any support or help she may need if staff are not present.

Night-time currently is uncertain for Rachael as she feels vulnerable on her own. The neighbours downstairs have been noisy and this has disturbed her. Rachael has never called for help at night or left the house, but her parents are not sure that she is sleeping well and worry about her overnight.

What's not working now

- Staff recruitment: maintaining a full compliment of staff
- Obtaining cover when staff are sick
- Having noisy neighbours, and there being too much noise in general
- Having support provided at the same time every day regardless of what Rachael is doing or needs help with
- Rachael's mum still needing to be the person who drives and leads the team to do things for and with Rachael

- Mum and the family needing to step in when things go wrong with staffing arrangements
- Her parents' concerns that, as they get older, the focus on them leading and safeguarding the process for Rachael through the option of a Direct Payment Option is not sustainable

Matching people to work with Rachael

Because the recruitment and retention of staff has been difficult, Rachael's mum has written a list of the attributes for future members of Rachael's staff team. They should be:

- Quietly voiced
- Able to pace themselves
- Genuine people
- Caring people
- Patient
- Animated
- Sociable
- Positive
- Confident
- Funny
- Fun loving
- Imaginative
- Creative
- Accepting
- Good listeners
- Observant
- Sensitive

Staff should also be able to:

- Take their time, and give Rachael time, to do things
- Enjoy music and animals

- Join-in singing with Rachael
- Cook well
- Drive a car
- Crack a joke
- Take an interest in beauty stuff

Rachael's hopes and dreams

We spent time together thinking about what the dream would be for Rachael. Knowing what Rachael's hopes and dreams are helps Rachael, and those who know and love her, to build life opportunities and support her towards those dreams every day. Here are the things we came up with:

- Having purpose and giving back to others
- Being happy in my house
- Having a job, or my own business, offering manicures, pedicures, foot massage etc
- Being in a loving relationship
- Marriage
- Meeting friends and being a good friend to others
- Hosting parties
- Having fun
- Performing and singing
- Having a dog or a cat
- Being more independent having more freedom
- Getting help when needed flexibly around my changing life!

Outcomes

We used all the information we gathered through the planning process to work out six big things that really matter in Rachael's life: the things that she wants to achieve for herself now and in the future. These outcomes describe the destination Rachael wants to reach; the way in which her Individual Service Fund is used as the vehicle to help her get there must always reflect these outcomes.

Outcome 1: *I have a real purpose to help others*

My quality of life will improve because I will have things to do

My skills and confidence will improve because I will have things to do

Outcome 2: *I look great everyday*

My quality of life will improve because I will stay as well as I can

My confidence and morale will improve

Outcome 3: *I am making other people happy and relaxed*

My quality of life will improve because I will be seeing more people

My confidence and skills will improve

Outcome 3: *I am safe at night*

My quality of life will improve because I will feel safe

My confidence, morale and skills will improve

Outcome 5: *I spend time with friends and people I like*

My quality of life will improve because I will be seeing more people

My confidence and skills will improve

Outcome 6: *I get to spend time on my own in my house*

My quality of life will improve because I will be living the way I want

My confidence and skills will improve

Vehicle

3. Vehicle

We have our bearings and you have painted a personal picture of the future you want to have and the destination you want to reach. In the next section we will think about the route you are going to take to get there. But before we do that you will need to think about the vehicle you want to choose to take you on this journey.

Just as you have options about your home and your community, you also have options about how much freedom you think you can manage, and how much control you want to take over the day-to-day arrangements for your life. These options are set out in act of parliament, the *Social Care (Self-directed Support) (Scotland) Act* 2013, and in the statutory guidance that comes with it. There are four options described in the Act and we will have a look below at what these options are and how they differ from each other. Whichever option you choose, however, there will need to be fuel in the tank, and this comes in the form of your Individual Budget (the money the local authority or health and social care partnership (HSCP) is willing to allocate to be spent on the help you get a good life). Your local statutory services authority should let you know at the earliest stage possible what the size of this Individual Budget is likely to be, as this will make it much easier for you to plan your journey home without worrying if you have enough fuel to take you on the route you choose.

Option 1 provides you with the greatest amount of control and allows you to have a **Direct Payment**. If you choose this vehicle then your Individual Budget will be paid directly into a bank account that you, or someone acting on your behalf, will manage in accordance with the agreed plan for your support. You will then be responsible for using this money to employ any paid staff you require and to meet any other costs contained in the plan to make sure you get a good life. A Direct Payment is a more 'hands-on' vehicle – and you will have to do nearly all of the driving yourself. But this is the way to go if you want to have the maximum amount of control over every aspect of your life and, for that reason, this is the approach that many have long advocated in the disability movement. You will also have a lot of responsibility – for managing the Direct Payment bank account and for recruiting, employing and

managing the paid staff you require. But across the country you will find that there is a lot of help available to assist you or your family in managing these responsibilities, through 'Centres for Inclusive Living' and similar organisations. Website references for the Centres for Inclusive Living in Glasgow and Edinburgh are included at the close of this section.

If you want to carry a bit less responsibility but still retain a large element of control, then you can choose Option 2 which allows you to have an **Individual Service Fund**. An Individual Service Fund allows you to take a more flexible approach, where you retain some elements of direct control while working in partnership with others who manage some aspects of your support arrangements on your behalf. For example:

- you might want to retain responsibility for managing the Individual Budget and the bank account, while delegating responsibility for the employment and management of staff to a social care agency;
- or, you might want the reverse arrangement – where you remain the employer and manager of staff, but delegate the financial management of the individual Budget to a social care organisation or to some other entity or individual.

It is also possible for you to retain your **Direct Payment** and for you or your family to contract with an organisation providing you with support to manage all or a part of the Direct Payment as an **Individual Service Fund**.

So if you go down the road with an Individual Service Fund you will be travelling in a 'dual control' vehicle. You will have a variety of levers and switches at your disposal as you try to find the right balance of control and responsibility for you. For more information about what to expect with an Individual Service Fund you might want to have a look at the guide to Individual Service Funds published by the Centre for Welfare Reform (Smith & Brown, 2018).

Option 3 gives you the least amount of control and the least amount of responsibility: this is the **Care Management** approach, a vehicle with more 'automatic transmission' built in. You still choose your destination and decide upon the type of life you want to lead, but you ask the local authority or the HSCP to manage your Individual Budget and all other financial matters, and ask them to employ and manage any paid staff

you may need or commission these services from a social care organisation on your behalf.

These are three basic models of vehicle at your disposal. Whichever one you choose, you will still want to customise it as much as possible so that it fits you as personally as possible. You might even want to think about Option 4, your very own 'hybrid vehicle' containing elements of all three approaches – Direct Payment, Individual Service Fund or Care Management – and there should be help on hand from local professionals to help you do this.

REFERENCES

Pages 42-45 offer a real world example of an Individual Service Fund. This plan has been shared with the permission of Rachael and her family.

Glasgow Centre for Inclusive Living http://www.gcil.org.uk

Lothian Centre for Inclusive Living https://www.lothiancil.org.uk

Social Care (Self-directed Support) (Scotland) Act 2013.

Social Care (Self-directed Support) (Scotland) Act 2013: Statutory Guidance.

Smith S & Brown F (2018) *Individual Service Funds: a guide to making Self-Directed Support work for everyone*. Sheffield, Centre for Welfare Reform.

Rachael's Individual Service Fund

The amount available for Rachael's individual budget is £73,908. Rachael and her family want to have the budget managed for them by a Third Party, as an Individual Service Fund (ISF). The service provider has experience of managing ISFs, is willing to take on this responsibility and will therefore hold, manage and account for the budget on Rachael's behalf.

Personal assistants

Rachael will have her own staff identified to work with her specifically and funded from the ISF. Staff will be flexible around Rachael's life as it changes rather than tied to predetermined, rigid hours of support. Personal Assistants will spend more time helping Rachael focus on how she can develop the things she needs and wants in her life. They will also concentrate on her personal care and hygiene, and help her to develop and learn new skills.

Time spent with family and friends

As Rachael has a full life with lots of people who love her, she currently spends time with her family without support staff. This happens at regular times throughout the year, and these times have been clearly identified to ensure they are reflected within the overall package of support available to Rachael. They are equivalent to 630 hours per year, or an annual "saving" of £10,050.

Regular support hours

These hours will be used each day to enable Rachael to be supported with her day to day living activities, keeping her healthy, well and safe, supporting her to meet her outcomes and live a full life. Some hours can be used flexibly to meet changing needs, e.g in relation to illness. A total of 72.5 regular hours of support will be required each week, equivalent to an annual cost of £60,169.

Work buddy

We will look for a work-buddy as part of the team or someone may be employed specifically to take on this role with Rachael. This person must be interested and passionate about the same things as Rachael in her work pursuits. These hours will be taken from the regular support hours described above but will offer a very specific focus in meeting Rachael's outcomes.

Citizen enablement worker

The person in this new role will carry responsibility for planning, meeting people, making connections for Rachael, researching opportunities, and generally implementing her plan. The role will ensure that these tasks do not continue to be the responsibility of Rachael's mum. 4hrs per week will be allocated for this role, equating to £3,389 per annum. It may be that the time used and/or the hours paid used are not always spent with Rachael directly.

Support when away on holiday

Rachael loves going away on holiday with her friends, and when she goes on holiday the support she requires is different from when she is at home. She pays for the cost of the holiday itself from her own finances. The cost of support needs to be adjusted when she is away, however, and needs to include the cost for staff sleeping over, amounting to £966 per year.

Overnight contingency costs

One of Rachael's main anxieties is that something may go wrong during the night. Even with assistive technology in place, it is important for Rachael to feel that, if she needed it, someone could stay over with her (for example, when she is ill, or the technology has broken down). We have calculated a conservative flexible contingency budget for 14 nights per year, equating to an annual amount of £966.

On-call costs

Call-Connect will provide reassurance and contact via computer. If, however, Rachael requires additional support, or for some reason has a problem, *Call-Connect* will call Rachael's parents who live nearby and can respond. When they are on holiday a staff member will be on-call overnight and available to respond. The annual cost will be £588.

Non staff-related costs

There has been some concern about Rachael being at home alone, particularly at night. Her parents are worried that the current call system is neither safe nor responsive enough for Rachael. To provide additional reassurance, *Call Connect* can be used to support Rachael when staff are not there in the evening and during the night. This will offer an interactive, layered service which can be purchased and changed as necessary. The total annual cost will be £4,812.

Paying for a cleaner

Rachael will benefit from a cleaner to keep her house in great condition. This will be cost-effective, freeing personal assistants from having to carry out this role. This will be funded from Rachael's ISF at a cost of approximately £1,152 per year.

Training

It is planned to use Rachael's talents and gifts to help her developing more meaningful opportunities to give back to her community, or to work and earn money, through her own pop-up manicure and Tai foot massage business. Total training costs for this are estimated at £1,840 per annum.

BUDGET ALLOCATED = £73, 908

SPENDING PROPOSED	AMOUNT
Support Hours	£60,169
Citizen Enablement Worker	£3,389
Support on holiday	£966
Overnight contingency	£966
On-call	£588
Non staff costs	£4,812
Cleaner	£1,152
Training	£1,840
TOTAL	**£73,882**

Road map

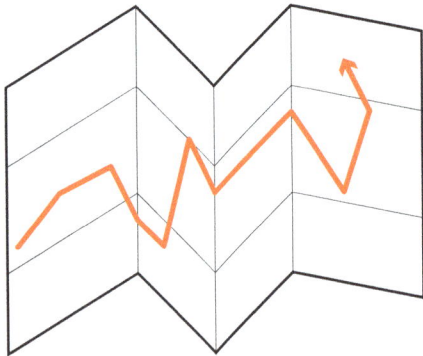

4. Road Map

We have our *bearings*, together with a picture of your preferred *destination*. And your chosen vehicle awaits, with fuel in the tank. We now need a *road map* showing how you are going to get there. This stage is about how to make the picture of your desirable future spring into life and become a reality. You may hear people refer to this as your Support Plan. So, it should contain everything you and others need to know to make sure you are able to lead a full and meaningful life back home.

The road map will cover all of these bases:

- **your house and home;**
- **the help you will require to live at home;**
- **the people who will help you live at home;**
- **the money you will need to live at home.**

Plotting Your Route

If you are picking up this guide afresh at this point it might be worth having a look back at Part 2. This talks about how you might go about describing the plan that you have for your own life back home, and how you might go about painting a picture of the life that you choose for yourself.

We are beginning here to turn our attention towards the kind of help you might need to bring that picture to life. Remember that in painting a picture of who you are and what you want, you may already have started to collect some important information about the help you are going to need. There is bound to be some overlap between the two stages. As before, when you were describing the life that you want back home, you will again need all the important people in your life coming together and working together with you as a team. So you will need the people who love you and

know you really well and the professional people who have some responsibility for you both where you live now and where you will live in the future.

And again, you also need to remember that there are people around the country, in different organisations, who are available to help you plot your route. It can be a great advantage to have an **independent** facilitator with lots of experience, who is good at personal planning, helping you, and all the people who are important to you, to get this right. Once again, you might want to bear in mind the fact that there are many organisations in different parts of Scotland where you will find people who are able to help in this way. Please see Citizen Network, In Control Scotland and Person Centred Planning Network Scotland websites for more information.

There are some professional people it will be important for you to get to know during this time. The specific roles that they occupy may be crucial in making sure that your journey home is completed successfully. They are likely to include:

- a **Discharge Co-ordinator**, based either where you live now or in the community you are returning to;

- a named **Advocate** to work on your behalf - an advocate is someone who works for you, and whose job it is to get your point of view across to others, to give you a voice - especially when there is a disagreement between what you wish for yourself and what other people think is best for you; an advocate should be someone free from any conflicts of interest;

- a named **Responsible Clinician** – a medical person, most likely a psychiatrist, whose job it is to authorise your discharge, and to make sure any medication you have is fully reviewed before you leave the place you are living in;

- a **Social Worker** from the local area you are returning to, who, amongst other things, will help you get reconnected to the local community and make the most of the opportunities there.

House and home

If you have been moved away from home you do not yet have a house or a place to call home. And this is a very important thing to have remedied.

In order to be able to turn your picture of home into reality, and to find the house you are looking for, it is important that you have access to the full range of housing options that are open to other adults citizens. Housing Options Scotland is a good source of information about what is available to you.

If you have said that you want to return to live with a member or members of your family, this is something you will have fully examined, explored and agreed with them at the stage where you were painting a picture of your future life. If this has been agreed then you may not need to find a new house. It may be possible for you to move into the house they currently live in. But you will need to make sure that there is enough room in the house for you so that you will be able to have your own bedroom. There may also need to be changes or adaptations made to the house so that it is suitable for you, especially if you have a physical disability or if your mobility is restricted in any way. If the existing house cannot be adapted to suit you, the family as a whole may need to find a new place to stay.

There will also need to be discussions about whether or not you will have any security of tenure in these circumstances, and whether or not anything can be done to provide you with some.

If you have said that you want to live alone, or with another person who does not have their own home, your options for finding your new house in your preferred home town or area will include:

- renting from a private landlord;
- renting from a public sector landlord, such as a Housing Association or a Local Authority; and
- owning your own home.

Housing officers, social workers and others will be able to give you advice about what might be available to rent or buy in your home area. You will have to match that information against the idea of home you have described in your picture. You

will probably find it useful to take this information and have it made into a housing specification written up to help with this search for a house that you can afford, with the right kind of design and in a part of town that makes sense for you to live in. It will be important to find out who the housing providers are in the local area and to determine which of these are able and willing to work in partnership with you to make sure your search for somewhere to live is successful. Housing providers can also help you think through any one-off adaptations that may be required to make the house suitable for you, and how they might be paid for.

Buying your own house

Buying your own house is a complicated matter, and is not always the best option for everyone. Very often you can get a good housing deal for yourself simply by renting. If house ownership is the best option for you, however, then it is important to remember that the housing costs element of Universal Credit can include help towards the interest payments on mortgages, repairs, and home improvements. Again, Housing Options Scotland can help you get the best advice about all this.

Renting your house

If you end up owning your own house then, of course, no one can put you out of that house, unless you stop paying the mortgage!

Things are different if you rent a house, and there are different rules depending on whether you are living in a privately rented house or in social housing (where you rent from a public body). It is important for your own long-term security and peace of mind that if you choose to rent a house you get the most **secure tenancy** possible.

In Scotland there are several different kinds of tenancy, and the rights you will have as a tenant will depend on which type you have.

A **tenancy agreement** is an agreement between you and your landlord (the owner of the property) that describes your rights to live in a rented property.

If you are a **private tenant** and you are the only person living in the house you will have a **private residential tenancy**. This is a new type of tenancy that came into

force in Scotland in December 2017, replacing assured and short assured tenancies. agreements for all new tenancies.

Your landlord must provide you with a either a written or an electronic copy of your tenancy agreement within 28 days of the start of the tenancy. The Scottish Government has published a **model tenancy** your landlord can use to establish the agreement and this describes the rights and responsibilities of both the tenant and the landlord. If your landlord does not use the model tenancy the private residential tenancy statutory terms must still be included in your tenancy agreement.

If you **share a private flat or house with other people**, you will have one of these tenancies:

- in a **Joint tenancy** everyone living in the flat or house has the same agreement and shares responsibility for paying the rent and bills. If one person doesn't pay, the others will have to pay it.
- in a **Sole tenancy** one person signs the agreement and is responsible for paying the rent and bills. Everyone else still has to pay their fair share, but if someone doesn't pay, the person who signed is responsible for coming up with the money.
- in a **Separate tenancy** everyone in the house has a separate tenancy agreement and is responsible for paying the amount of rent stated in the agreement.

If you are a **social housing tenant** - the tenant of a property belonging to a local authority, a housing association or housing co-op - you will probably have either a **Scottish secure tenancy** (SST) or a **short Scottish secure tenancy** (SSST).

Centre for Welfare Reform

The help you will need to live at home

You are going to need the right type of help to allow you to live well in your new home. The picture you have drawn of your preferred destination will help you work out:

- the types of different support you are going to need from other people; and
- how much of these different types of support you are going to need, which times of day you are going to need it, and on which days of the week.

As you start your journey back home from a long-stay institution it is very likely that you will carry with you a negative reputation and a perception that you present very high risks to yourself and/or other people.

For these reasons the levels of support other people think you require are likely to be very high, especially at the outset. It is important to remember that it is very likely that these high levels of support will not be required in the long-term, and that it is very likely that they can be reduced on a staged basis over time.

As before, you will probably need assistance from other people in working all this out. Perhaps the people who helped you draw up the plan. Or perhaps some of the people who helped draw up the plan together with other people who are going to have an important part to play when you get home. Maybe some people who have not been involved up to this point, but who have good experience of helping people design their support.

Use the picture of the life you want to have back home to begin to list the **things that other people might need to help you to manage well**. Remember that at this stage you are thinking about the help you will need, not so much about who will provide it. We will come to this shortly. Try not to think about the solutions just yet.

- Some people need help to manage very **personal things** like hygiene, dressing, eating, continence, transferring from being seated to standing up, and vice versa. If you need help with some or all of these things, make a list of them. Then do some thinking about the type of help you need for each of them: what exactly is it that other people need to do to help you manage these things? And how often does this happen – many times a day, or just once a day or maybe less?

- Some people need help to manage **household things** like preparing meals, doing housework, managing money. Again, if you need help with some or all of these things, get them written down. Then, once more, do some thinking about the type of help you need for each of them: what exactly is it that other people need to do to help you manage these things? And how often does this happen – many times a day, or just once a day or maybe less?

- Some people need help to manage **healthcare things** like taking medication, or sticking to a special diet. So, if you need help with these things, make a list, and again work out what exactly it is that other people need to do to help you, and how often this is required.

- Some people need help to manage **social things** like getting out of the house, getting on and off buses, getting in and out of cars, going shopping, going to restaurants and cinemas, visiting other people's homes, etc. If you need help these things, try to list them and try to say exactly what it is that other people need to do to help you manage these things? It may be more difficult to say how often these things will happen, but give it a go.

- Some people need help because of things that they do that **risk their health and wellbeing** through things that they do, or do not do. If you need help for this reason, in order to keep you safe and well, it is important to describe in some details the things that you do and don't do that put you at risk in this way, and the things that the person helping you should do to make sure you remain safe and well. These descriptions might look something like: *'when a particular thing is happening or not happening, this probably means that I am likely to put myself at risk by doing a, or b, or c, and if this is the case then the person helping me should respond by doing e, f, or g.'*

Centre for Welfare Reform

- Some people need help because of things that they do that risk the health and wellbeing of others – again through things that they do, or do not do. If you need help for this reason, in order to keep other people safe and well, it is important to describe in some detail the things that you do and don't do that put others at risk in this way, and the things that the person helping you should do to make sure other people remain safe and well. These descriptions might look something like: *'when a particular thing is happening or not happening, this probably means I am likely to put others at risk by doing a, or b, or c; if this is the case then the person helping me should respond by doing e, f, or g.'*

Once you have thought about all of these things the various strands will need to be pulled together into **a plan that summarises all the help you will need**.

Now and later

It is often the case that people need more help when they first come home, and less later, when they have had an opportunity to settle into their new surroundings.

So it may be helpful, and sometimes necessary, to have a Support Plan in three parts describing:

1. The total amount of **all the help** you will need at the start.
2. A **reduced amount of help** you think you will need after a few weeks, or months, depending on your circumstances.
3. How the **transition** between these two points in your support arrangements will be phased.

The cost of the plan

As you start to describe the amount of help you will need to live your life back home you will have in mind the amount of money you have in your individual budget. Knowing this amount of money in advance will help you make sure that you get the fullest benefit from the money available to you. You will need to be especially aware

of the price you are likely to have to pay for any paid support that you build into your plan. The person facilitating the plan with you will be able to help you work all this out.

Once you have come to the end of the support planning process you need to be able to work out the cost of the plan. It is unlikely that the cost of your support will remain the same forever, and if your plan has made allowance for more help at the beginning and less later, then, again, you should know the cost of these two stages of the plan. Making this transition may require some one-off amounts of spending to be approved as part of the plan.

You may come to the conclusion with the people around you that, no matter how you try to adjust the plan, the amount of money in your individual budget is not going to be enough to allow you to have the help you need to live life fully and safely. In these circumstances it will be necessary for you to go back to the people in the local authority or HSCP who allocated your budget to request to have it adjusted, in the light of the evidence you have gathered through the planning process.

The people who will help you to live at home

Now that you are clear about the help you will need, and when you will need it, you can come back to do some thinking about how you will get that help. Who are the people who are going to support you in this way?

It may be best to start by thinking about **family members** and **friends** who might be able and willing to provide some of the support you need. There may also be **volunteers** and existing **organisations and activities** in your home community that can help with some of what you need. If you have been away from home for some time, however, you may not be able, at least at first, to rely on family, friends and community in this way. Remember also that you may be able to use your budget to buy some non-recurring items of technology, or to employ people who undertake specific tasks such as cleaning or laundry.

Even if you are very well connected within your family and community, and have lots of friends, it is still very likely that you will need to get some of your help, and perhaps the majority of it, from **paid staff**. The way in which this paid support is organised

and paid for will depend on the vehicle you have chosen for directing your own support. Once more, you will be able to gain assistance in choosing service providers committed to social inclusion through the Citizen Network website.

Whichever vehicle you have chosen, however, there are some important principles about how paid staff should come into your life:

- paid staff work for you – even if they are employed by someone else, they first and foremost work for you, and are accountable to you;
- you must be content that anyone coming to work for you is a good match with you, your personality, and your interests – someone you feel you can get along with and who seems to have a genuine interest in how you want to live your life; you may find it useful to have a **person specification** prepared to help with the search for these people;
- there must also be time taken to prepare paid staff before they start working for you, so that they understand their role, are have all the information and skills required to carry it out;
- staff who are paid to work for you also need support themselves, to help them keep on track and to do the best job they can- it is important that whoever is employing them is equipped to provide this type of support and any necessary training;
- whoever their employer is they should have a **job description** and a **contract of employment** that make clear they work specifically for you.

The money you will need to live at home

Social Security Benefits

You are going to need money to live on when you get back home. If you are not going to have a job when you first get back home, and if you don't have a lot of money of your own, you will need to make sure you get all the income you are entitled to from social security benefits. You need to make sure that you have a full **benefits check** undertaken. Your Social Worker or a Welfare Rights Officer may be able to help with this, or you may be able to get the help you need from the Child Poverty Action Group or your local Citizens Advice Scotland Bureau.

If you qualify for social security benefits you will probably qualify for **Universal Credit**. You will need this to pay for both your housing costs and your ordinary living expenses. Universal Credit is a means-tested benefit for people of working-age who are on a low income. It replaces six older means-tested benefits: Income Support, Income-based Jobseeker's Allowance, Income-related Employment and Support Allowance, Housing Benefit, Child Tax Credit and Working Tax Credit. Universal Credit is paid on a monthly basis. Entitlement is worked out by comparing the basic amount of money that the government says you need to live on with your personal financial resources.

There is also a **housing costs element** of Universal Credit. This money is to help you with your housing costs. If you are a tenant it can help with rent and some service charges. The amount you get will be calculated differently depending on whether you are a **private tenant** or a **social housing tenant**.

REFERENCES

Pages 58-65 offer examples of a real case study of a family who used an Individual Service Fund, a Housing Specification and a Transition Plan.

Child Poverty Action Group https://cpag.org.uk/scotland/welfare-rights

Citizens Advice Scotland https://www.citizensadvice.org.uk/scotland/

Citizen Network https://citizen-network.org

Housing Options Scotland https://www.housingoptionsscotland.org.uk

In Control Scotland https://www.in-controlscotland.org

The Smith Family

The Smith family used to live in a very difficult situation. Two of their sons, Robert and William had very significant learning difficulties and the same degenerative disease. They lived together, as a family of five, in a two bedroom house with only the most minimal support. Eventually, when the family reached breaking point, they put both boys in a hospital unit and refused to take them home.

The NHS and Social Services accepted that they had an obligation to provide a jointly funded service to the two boys and so began by asking an independent organisation, Inclusion Glasgow, to develop two single residential services for the boys (which were each expected to cost £90,000 per year). Their assumption was that the family could not support their two boys and that the 'challenging behaviour' that the boys displayed could only be managed in an expensive residential support service.

The first thing that Inclusion Glasgow did was to gather more information about the boys and their family, using a process called Essential Lifestyle Planning and also to get the family to tell their own story in their own words (see Figure 5).

The second thing Inclusion Glasgow did was to write a service proposal that set out the assumptions upon which a new service should be designed for the Smith family. Three of the most important of those assumptions were that the family needed:

1. regular on-going support, but support they could control.
2. to move into a new house that was adapted to meet their needs.
3. a better respite service.

This service proposal was agreed in principle and Social Work and the NHS agreed to jointly fund the new service, at a cost of £30,000 per year for each boy. Inclusion Glasgow organised all of the money which it received to provide support as an Individual Service Fund an identified fund of money ring-fenced and managed solely for the use of the boys to receive the support that they needed and other things that would help them get a good life.

Finding the family appropriate support became the first problem that needed a practical solution.

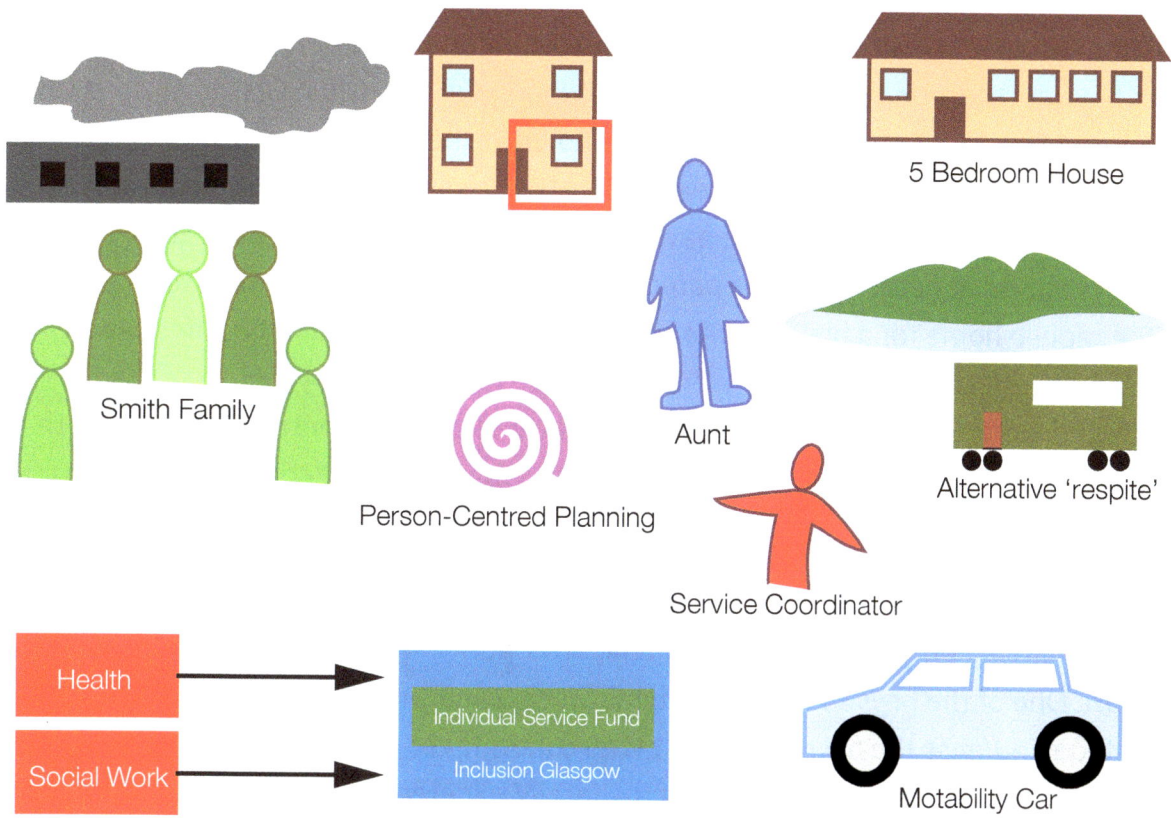

FIGURE 5. THE SMITH FAMILY STORY

Inclusion Glasgow suggested that the family think about people they knew who might be able to help them. The family were reluctant to have strangers involved as they would need to spend a great deal of time in the family home and because of this they chose to employ a close family member to give them the support they needed and they are able to control this support on a day to day basis.

The second problem was resolved by agreeing a different payment schedule with the NHS and then by transforming some of the revenue funding into a capital grant that could be given to the family. Legal agreements were also made between Inclusion Glasgow, the family and the NHS to ensure that there was enough security for each party. The family worked effectively and quickly to find a new house which suited the needs of their boys and they located the right house which they have now lived in for 14 years.

The last major part of the service that needed to change was the respite service. The existing residential respite service cost £1,000 per week, per boy, and it refused to take both boys at the same time (they were 'too challenging'). Inclusion Glasgow asked the family to think about the kind of breaks and holidays they really valued. When they realised how expensive the respite service was they replaced it by hire-purchasing a mobile home by the sea; this home gave the family much more flexibility. Sometimes the boys stayed at home while the parents had a break away; sometimes the boys went to the mobile home for a break by the sea. The family were able to enjoy life together much more effectively when they were able to live in a house that met all of their needs and were able to use their funding available to them to control the supports that they needed. The family became stronger and no longer merely dependent on others.

Over the last 14 years Inclusion Glasgow has continued to hold an Individual Service Fund (ISF) on the family's behalf. Inclusion Glasgow manages the money and takes responsibility for employing Judy who is the boys' auntie; offering her training and support. One of the boys sadly died some years ago and the individual budget was adjusted to address the needs of Robert who continues to get the support he needs. The Individual Service Fund (ISF) allows the family to determine when they get support how much support they get and they manage all of this on a day to day basis. They have continued to plan around Roberts needs sharing dreams and hopes for the future and using the ISF creatively to achieve these.

Inclusion Glasgow takes responsibility for accounting for the money and gives the family regular information on what is being used and discusses with them how they want to continue to use the money they have available. The caravan has long since gone but the family are now needing to extend Robert's room due to his changing needs and some of the ISF money has been spent on building a small summer room extension to his bedroom which Robert loves spending time in.

This very individual arrangement gives the family the control they need and want over who supports their son, how they spend the budget and allows them to balance their son's needs with their own needs. They have all the control, flexibility and choice they want without some of the anxieties and stresses of managing the money directly and being an employer. Robert has thrived and continues to live a full life at the centre of his loving family.

Housing Specification

This is an example from Housing Options Scotland: you may be asked, or helped, to complete something similar to assist in the search for your new home.

In which area do you want to live?			
Who would be living with you?			
How many bedrooms do you need and what features should the house have?			
Have you registered your housing needs with the Council?	Yes	No	
Have you registered your housing needs with any Housing Associations or Co-operatives?	Yes	No	
What other steps have you taken to find a suitable home?			
How much, if anything, could friends or family contribute to assist you financially to buy?	£		
Would another family member or friend, consider buying a property to let to you if you could repay them with rent through Housing Benefit?	Yes	No	
Will you find your home hard to heat?	Prefer not to say	Yes	No
Do you worry about fuel bills?	Prefer not to say	Yes	No

Centre for Welfare Reform

Thomas's Transition Plan

Introduction

Thomas is a young man who for the past three years has been living in the Forest Green specialist assessment unit, some 150 miles distant from the town of Littlesford, where he grew up, and where members of his family still live. Plans have now been made for him to return to a home of his own in Littlesford, with support being provided by the organisation Community Impact.

Thomas experiences anxiety and frustration and often expresses this through behaviour which is physically challenging to other people. Support arrangements have been designed to help Thomas manage this behaviour, but also to help him gradually take more control over his life, with his level of support reducing gradually over time.

Individual budget

To begin with, Thomas will receive support from two members of staff at all times (including overnight). The cost of providing this level of support to Thomas is in the region of £190,000 per year, similar to the cost of his placement at Forest Green. His home local authority, however, has set an indicative annual budget of £112,000 to be achieved by the close of a two year transition period. In addition, a one-off non-recurring amount of £60,000 has been agreed to facilitate this transition.

An individual service fund

The local authority has also determined that instead of providing funding for Thomas's service directly to Community Impact, on the basis of a spot purchase contract, an Individual Service Fund is being put in place, offering Thomas and his family greater control, creativity and flexibility in the design and delivery of support. With a high level of support and perceived high risk, the focus will be on keeping Thomas safe and well however an ISF will allow for flexibility and will be used more creatively over time to enable Thomas to have a good life not just a service, having it in place now is crucial.

Personal plan

A tailored person-centred plan has been developed for Thomas, introducing gradual change over the agreed period of time. The plan demonstrates how the need for intense 2:1 support will be reduced as Thomas increases his ability to manage the issues he faces and have a good life.

The changes will have a greater chance of being effective because considerable emphasis will be placed on Thomas feeling safe and developing trust with the support team who will get to know him well. At each stage changes will be agreed and confirmed by Thomas and his family with the inter-agency team (local authority, health service and service provider) involved with Thomas's support. There are three stages to this plan:

Stage 1 (0-6 months)

Once Thomas has settled into his home over the first few weeks, the first reduction in intense support will take place. From 6pm until 10pm each evening, 2:1 support will be replaced with 1:1 support. For the remainder of the first six month period, staff will "mirror" the behaviour of having one person supporting Thomas. This means that while one person is supporting Thomas, the second person will behave as if they were invisible, and nearer the end of the 6 month period will leave the house for short periods, staying available, however, able to respond immediately if required.

All change will be implemented gradually using this step down approach, demonstrating that any change is safe for Thomas and he is coping with the change before the change is confirmed.

After six months the effect of this reduction of support hours will be to reduce the annual budget to £169,000.

Stage 2 (7-12 months)

The safest time to make the next set of changes is likely to be during the night, when Thomas is asleep. The sleepover arrangement will be changed to a waking night arrangement. The awake night-time staff member will withdraw from the house, but will be able to respond quickly if needed. There will continue to be a back-up person in place once the night shift is withdrawn.

The impact on the budget of removing the waking night person and changing the sleepover to a waking night will be to reduce the annual budget to £135,000, with Thomas still living in the family home two days per week.

To summarise then, the impact on Thomas's budget over a full twelve month period:

- the cost for the first six months will be £84,500;
- the cost for the second six month period £67,500;
- the total cost for the full twelve month period will be £152,000 (contrasting with the previous annual cost of £190,000)
- £40,000 of the non-recurring £60,000 will have been used.

Stage 3 (13-15 months)

Further reductions in overall levels of support are planned from this point onwards.

In the course of the first three months of year 2, the plan will be to reduce the amount of 2:1 staffing to only six hours per day. This change will be made flexibly over the period. Thomas will be receiving support to achieve new goals and outcomes and he may experience stress in tackling new things. It is possible his health may also fluctuate, and it will be possible to increase support if and when this is required. By the end of the 15 month period the budget will have reduced to the equivalent of £143,000 per annum. A further £7,750 of the non-recurring £60,000 amount will have been used, amounting to a total of £47,750.

Stage 4 (16-24 months)

The remaining £12,250 of the non-recurring amount will be used to implement further changes in the following nine months. If Thomas continues to respond well to support strategies, to sleep well, and have a full and meaningful life, his service will be designed along the following lines:

1. Staff will support Thomas 1:1 within the home and for most occasions outwith the home, where he is familiar with his surroundings and activities.
2. There will be a flexible bank of 15 hours of 2:1 support available to be used either weekly when needed or if Thomas is unwell or needs additional support when on holiday;

3. On the basis that by this time Thomas will be settled in his home, with a regular sleep pattern, a normal sleepover arrangement will be in place.

4. On-call hours will continue to be built into the budget, permitting additional responses to be made if at any time necessary.

5. Thomas will spend time with his family freeing up some of his budget to be used for agreed outcomes. While supporting Thomas to be more in control and safe, it is also important that we support him to have a good life and a good relationship with his family and to develop new opportunities for friendships and experiences. For example: Thomas loves walking we plan to develop this gift by Thomas becoming part of a walking club and walking for charity. Through this Thomas will make lots of meaningful connections and have real purpose. Thomas loves to draw and is a fabulous artist, one of his outcomes is to sell his art in the future. Thomas's ISF will fund some Art tutoring and materials, it will support his publicity and allow him to share his art with others meeting his outcome in the future.

By the end of the second year with the right support in place, the budget will have reduced to the equivalent of £112,000 per annum. Thomas will be living a good life, be safe and well and his ISF will be funding outcomes to continue to help him achieve his dreams for the future.

Passport

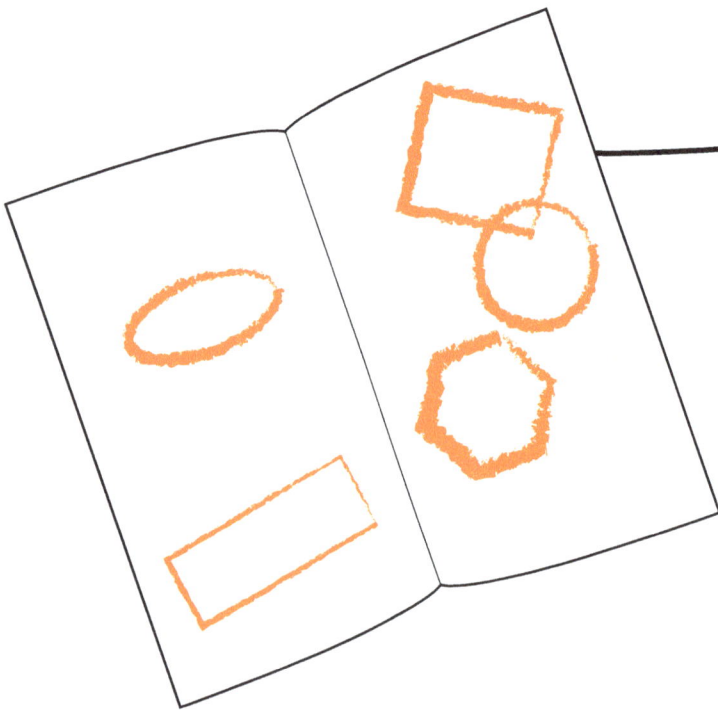

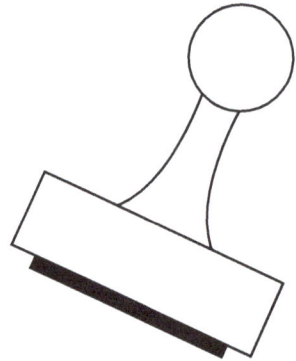

5. Passport

Congratulations! Now that your destination is clear, your *vehicle* is ready and your route has been planned, you are almost ready to make the journey. All that remains is to make sure that you take your *passport* with you.

Discharge plan

Before you leave the institution your Responsible Clinician, Social Worker and Discharge Co-ordinators are responsible for compiling a **Discharge Plan**. This is an important official document. It will be used to review how things are working out for you back home at the end of the first four weeks. So, together with your Advocate, you need to make sure that the Discharge Plan describes everything you will need to sustain your new life. This is your official passport certifying your identity and citizenship and entitling you to travel. Just like a traveller setting off for the airport, you won't get terribly far if the passport you take with you is out-of-date or belongs to someone else.

Partnership agreements

Finally, but vitally, in order for your passport to be completely valid, it must contain clear, **written commitments** from the various agencies involved providing you with the additional insurance that you are not likely to find yourself back in the same situation, a long way from home, at some point in the future.

There are three types of written commitment they must give you, and which you **MUST** ensure are included within the Discharge Plan.

They must commit to:

- **implement the support plan and the costings associated with it**; and, where the plan is to be phased, to implement those stages and costings;

- **work alongside you once you are home in a flexible, adaptable partnership**, reflecting the principle that your personal requirements will change over time and that your support arrangements will benefit from regular review, refreshment and renewal;

- **guarantee your right to remain in your own home for the long-term**, making sure that this right is neither superseded nor contradicted by any requirement you may have for 'compulsory measures of care', on account of your mental health or challenging behaviour.

Without these commitments your passport is little more than a short-term work permit and will not provide you with the level of security you need and deserve.

Documents

This is a checklist of all the **documents** and **processes** you will now have completed, having worked through the various stages of this travel guide. You will need to check that the Discharge Plan contains or refers to all of the things listed here.

Stage	Process	Document
Compass	Human Rights Orientation	
Destination	Person-Centred Planning	Life Plan
Vehicle	Setting the amount of your individual budget Choosing how you want to direct your support	Individual Budget Statement Self-Directed Support Agreement
Road Map	Support Planning	Housing Specification Tenancy Agreement Support Plan Person Specification Job Description Employment Contract Support Plan Costing Benefits Check Allocation of GP Medication Review [Ministry of Justice/Mental Health Tribunal Agreement, if required]
Passport	Confirming the committment of all concerned	Partnership Agreements

Afterword

Afterword

Who will hold them to account?

In Scotland, as in the rest of the UK, there was, from the 1990s onwards, a major policy shift - away from long-stay hospital provision for people with learning disabilities towards community-based supported accommodation. This shift was reflected initially in the long-stay 'hospital' closure programme which began to gain momentum in the mid-nineties and then became formal national policy in 2000 (as part of the first national learning disability strategy, *The Same As You?*). This had obvious and significant implications for those people within that hospital population who were described as having complex disabilities or who displayed behaviours which challenged services.

The policy shift had two main drivers.

In part it reflected an assertion of the wider disability equality movement of the right of individual men and women with disabilities to be included in their own communities, alongside their families and friends, and to have a home of their own. Over the next decade these rights had been much more clearly asserted and formally articulated through the United Nations Convention on the Rights of Persons with Disabilities. While the wide-ranging implications of the Convention's principles have not – then or now - been fully realised in our society, they delineate, when taken together with the *Human Rights Act* (1998), the 'human rights approach' to social care, an important aspect of which is a commitment to universality: i.e. that there is no- one to whom these rights do not apply, no-one who can be excluded from their implications of dignity, respect and inclusion.

But the policy shift also reflected a set of clearer understandings about what type of services actually provide an effective response to people with these 'complex' service requirements. Jim Mansell's landmark report for the Department of Health in

England set the policy tone for this area of work and established standards of good practice for health and social work commissioners which, although never formally adopted in Scotland, were influential here too. In terms similar to the recommendations of the *Coming Home* report Mansell spoke of making a better use of investment in order:

- "to develop and expand the capacity of local services for people with learning disabilities to understand and respond to challenging behaviour
- to provide specialist services locally which can support good mainstream practice as well as directly serve a small number of people with the most challenging needs."

Mansell urged commissioners to:

"stop using services which are too large to provide individualised support; serve people too far from their homes; and do not provide people with a good quality life in the home or as part of the local community, in favour of developing more individualised, local solutions which provide a good quality of life."

It is therefore of the greatest concern that, despite the fact that over the intervening years these ethical and good practice arguments have continued to underpin public policy pronouncements throughout the UK, a sizeable group of people regarded as complex and challenging continue to be sent away from their local communities in Scotland, as amply evidenced by the *No Through Road* and *Coming Home* reports.

Why this should be the case is difficult to understand.

While it is understandable that reducing levels of social care funding of the austerity years have raised anxieties about costs there is no evidence that out-of-area institutional living is cheaper; in fact it is typically more expensive.

And, while lack of competence and/or knowledge amongst some local authorities and HSCP commissioners is responsible for the perpetuation of the institutional model, there is clearly a great deal of knowledge and competence amongst commissioners the length and breadth of Scotland, surely sufficient to be harnessed through Social Work Scotland and COSLA to ensure best practice and public policy is adhered

to nationally. In addition, the proper implementation of the Self-Directed Support legislation should be helping to sustain the enduring right of individuals to retain their place within their own communities.

But in the absence of the consistent application of evidence-led practice, we are thrown back on Jim Mansell's challenging question noted in the introduction to this guide:

"The real solution... is to stop using these kinds of places altogether. Who will hold local health and social services to account to make that happen?"

While ultimately we are all accountable for ensuring that the human rights of our fellow citizens are respected, we have a current opportunity to seek the assertion of that accountability through the Government's review of adult social care, charged with responsibility for ensuring "Scotland provides consistently excellent support for people who use these services". We have known for some time what it takes to provide that excellent support for people with learning disabilities who are 'complex' and who challenge services.

Now is the time for the review to determine that:

- the recommendations of the *Coming Home* report must be implemented;
- a national community of practice must be established between the statutory authorities and the third sector to ensure excellent practice in the commissioning and delivery of community support;
- all available community housing options must be mobilised to accelerate the return of those currently institutionalised;
- there must be no further admissions to institutions or use out-of-area placements;
- there must be a sufficient investment of funds to facilitate this programme of change.

REFERENCES

Mansell J (2007) *Services for people with learning disabilities and challenging behaviour or mental health needs.* London, Department of Health.

Mental Welfare Commission for Scotland (2016) *No Through Road: People with Learning Disabilities in Hospital.* Edinburgh, Mental Welfare Commission.

Scottish Executive (2000) *The Same As You? A review of people with learning disabilities.*

Scottish Government (2018) *Coming Home: A Report on Out-of-Area Placements and Delayed Discharge for People with Learning Disabilities and Complex Needs.* Edinburgh, Scottish Government.

Scottish Government. Review of Adult Social Care
https://www.gov.scot/news/review-of-adult-social-care/

Scottish Government (2013) *Social Care (Self-directed Support) (Scotland) Act.*

UK Government (1998) *Human Rights Act*:

United Nations (2006) *Convention on the Rights of Persons with Disabilities.*

Citizen Network

This guide has been published in association with Citizen Network, an international movement to achieve citizenship for all. Citizen Network brings together all those around the world who want to overcome prejudice, poverty and powerlessness.

We believe in diversity and equality: every single individual is equal and our differences are something to be acknowledged, nurtured and celebrated.

Anyone or any group who believes in these values can join Citizen Network.

People with disabilities, particularly people with more complex needs or people with mental health problems, too often find themselves stripped of their status as citizens. They are excluded, placed in institutional hospitals, care homes or special unit, cut off from their family, friends and community. This is not just an abuse of human rights, it is a serious loss to all of us. We all belong and we must work together to ensure that everyone gets the chance to a life of meaning, freedom and contribution.

Find out more about Citizen Network, and please join us it's free:

Visit: www.citizen-network.org

Find us on LinkedIn: citizen-network

Follow us on twitter: @citizen_network

Find us on facebook: fb.me/citizennetwork

Publishing Information

A New Way Home (Scottish Edition) © Frances Brown and John Dalrymple 2021
Figures 1, 2, 3, 4 and 5 © Simon Duffy 2017

First published March 2021
ISBN print: 978-1-912712-33-5
80 pp.

A New Way Home (Scottish Edition) is published by the Centre for Welfare Reform.

The publication is free to download from:
www.centreforwelfarereform.org

About the Authors

Frances Brown

Frances's background is in mental health and learning disability nursing. She has worked for the NHS and a range of third sector organisations in Scotland. She was previously the Director of Inclusion Glasgow, and has most recently worked as an independent consultant specialising in self-directed support and service design.

John Dalrymple

John is a social worker who has worked in local authority and third sector learning disability services in Scotland since the early 1980s. He was previously Principal Officer (Learning Disability) for Strathclyde Regional Council, and co-founder of Support for Ordinary Living in North Lanarkshire.

Frances and John have worked together in various capacities over the past twenty years, first in the context of the Lennox Castle Hospital closure programme in the mid-nineties, and ten years later as the joint development officers of In Control Scotland. Frances Brown and John Dalrymple are the founders of the consultancy Radical Visions.

Website: www.radicalvisions.wpengine.com

Email: frances@radicalvisions.com

and john@radicalvisions.com

RADICAL VISIONS

Centre for Welfare Reform

The Centre for Welfare Reform is an independent think tank. Its aim is to transform the current welfare state so that it supports citizenship, family and community. It works by developing and sharing social innovations and influencing government and society to achieve necessary reforms.

We have produced this toolkit as our contribution to the ongoing battle for justice fought by people with disabilities and their families. The ideas described in this guide are based on the experiences of people who have spent decades helping people leave institutional care and establish themselves as citizens within their own communities. We hope it is useful to people, families and those professionals who choose to be their allies.

To find out more go to www.centreforwelfarereform.org

We produce a monthly email newsletter, if you would like to subscribe to the list please visit: bit.ly/subscribe-cfwr

Find us on LinkedIn: centre-for-welfare-reform

Follow us on twitter: @CforWR

Find us on Facebook: fb.me/centreforwelfarereform

www.ingramcontent.com/pod-product-compliance
Lightning Source LLC
Chambersburg PA
CBHW080902030426
42336CB00017B/2983